12/2.

Jim, Vivian, Jim + Kristin,

Merry Christmas to one of our most favorite families who happen to live in one of our most favorite places to visit !!! Some of our most enjoyable memories have been with all of you in New York.

Love,

Dorothy + Joe

The Empire State

Whenever I travel to far off places and folks ask me where I'm from I'll reply, New York, but quickly add, the mountain part — it's called, The Adirondacks. Inevitably the response is, you mean there are mountains in New York, Wow! You see, most people equate New York State with sky scrapers, taxi cabs and multitudes of humanity. But there is more, a great deal more to our Empire State. So, within these pages it is my special privilege to present a brief glimpse of the state's unique diversity. Its unusual characteristics evolve into a manifestation of several totally different regions — and that's what this book is all about.

Mountains indeed, hundreds of them and in winter their collective conglomeration resembles the Alps or some equally exotic range. See for yourself in the double page aerial view of the Adirondacks. Then there are great rivers, canyons and waterfalls. Niagara is famous around the world, visited by millions yearly. But little known OK Slip Falls is also part of New York State, plunging 200 feet into a remote ravine. Perhaps only a handfull penetrate the wilderness each year to view its thundering splendor. Through the pages of this book you can experience the essence of these magnificent spectacles.

The limitation of pages preclude showing all the amazing sights and fascinating places I've photographed during preparation of this project. Nor can the thrill of flying low in a single engine plane around the greatest metropolis on earth be measured with a few colored images. The magic of dawn striking the tip of Long Island's Montauk Point, or, skimming over myriads of tiny tufted islands in the St. Lawrence Seaway is simply a sensation to be experienced. It is my hope that these photographs convey a portion of that exciting experience. Each image is an adventure unto itself with its own separate story, and may in some instances cause the observer to wonder, how in the world did he get that picture?

Often it is a matter of pure luck — of being in the right place at the right time. But more often than not it's purely perseverance. Of waiting out several days of rain or dense fog without a single frame being shot. Still others are the result of temporarily frozen fingers and feet in order to capture an image on film. I'm often asked, what kind of a camera do you use? That's a bit like asking an artist, what kind of a paintbrush do you use? The camera is simply a mechanical extension of being at the right place. But for those who really need to know, I use a Nikon along with all Nikon lenses. Also, the film is Kodachrome 64, manufactured right here in good old New York State.

Finally, and most importantly, the work represented here is also the result of many helpful individuals and contacts along the way. I am grateful to all those who assisted me with suggestions, or provided a "base camp" along the way. But I especially want to thank my friend and editor, James B. Patrick, who continues to have faith in my efforts with this my fourth book for FOREMOST PUBLISHERS. There are more to come folks!

Clyde H. Smith

Overleaf: Atlantic Ocean at eastern tip of Long Island, Montauk Point.

Photographs © copyright 1986 Clyde H. Smith
Copyright © 1986 Foremost Publishers, Inc.
This book, or portions thereof, may not be reproduced
in any form without the permission of Foremost Publishers,
Inc. Photographs may not be reproduced in any form
without the permission of Clyde H. Smith.
Edited by James B. Patrick
Designed by Donald G. Paulhus
Printed in Japan
ISBN 0-89909-096-6
Published by Foremost Publishers, Inc.
An affiliate of Yankee Publishing Inc.
Dublin, NH 03444

NEW YORK

The State

Photography by Clyde H. Smith
Introduction by Lionel Atwill

Published by Foremost Publishers, Inc.
An Affiliate of Yankee Publishing Inc.

Thread around an Empire

A dozen years ago, maybe more, a New York magazine ran on its cover a drawing of an aerial view of the United States. What made that cover unusual was the perspective: the drawing showed the country as a New Yorker — a Manhattanite — might perceive it: Long Island loomed largely in the foreground, Manhattan took up 80 percent of the picture, upstate New York and the Adirondacks accounted for most of the northern reaches, and everything else — New Jersey to Texas to California — was but a thin strip of wasteland between The Hudson River and the Pacific.

That cover was very popular. Someone printed it as a poster, which still hangs on many a Manhattan loft's wall. Manhattanites liked it because it *was* exactly how some of them saw the country: New York as the beginning and end of civilized life. (And those with more worldly views inevitably had such fierce loyalty to their city that a slight distortion of geographic reality was perfectly fine — even admirable.)

Upstaters (which is the vernacular for those who live in every part of New York outside of the five boroughs of the city) liked it because the artwork was, to their eye, cartoonish enough to poke a little fun at those seemingly eccentric, somewhat parochial city dwellers.

That cover comes to mind now because as I think about New York, the idea of the State being, if not *the* country, then a country, fascinates me. Another hazy memory bolsters my interest. I remember once hearing a radio ad from the New York State Department of Commerce. It noted that if New York were a separate country, its Gross National Product would place it tenth in a ranking of world economic powers. The Empire State could well be an *empire* of its own.

Mind you, it's not just the economic muscle of the State I find so interesting (and if it were, Californians would be quick to point out that *their* state would place eighth in that ranking, pushing New York back a place). What catches my imagination is the notion that New York is so diversified, not just in crops and business and manufacturing, but in land and people and ways of life, that it probably should be thought of in the way we think about countries rather than states. A town in the Adirondacks, after all — a Jay or a Keene or a Willsboro, where I lived for a good slice of my life — is as different from Albany or Buffalo, and certainly from Manhattan, as Paris is from Bombay.

Such diversity makes for a complex, fascinating state, although at times it can cause some confusion and misunderstanding, too. (Can a grape grower in the Finger Lakes sympathize with a subway conductor in Brooklyn? Does a Tupper Lake lumberjack appreciate the skills of a singing waiter in the Catskills? Might a glass blower at the Steuben plant in Corning share a Montauk charter boat captain's affection for Block Island Sound?) Certainly, that broad spectrum of New York's land and people and life may have hampered the growth of state patriotism, the sort of jingoism that can bring Texans to their feet on hearing the first few bars of "The Eyes of Texas."

But that is not to say New Yorkers are without loyalties and passion. To the contrary, they are loaded with it, but their loyalties are to town and neighborhood, to county or city rather than to state. New Yorkers are insulated by culture and topography, which leads to a fascinating Catch-22 situation: the very abundance of local loyalty and the absence of a dominant state pride are the very things that preserve and enhance New York's diversity . . . and make the state so appealing.

My theory about why this diversity continues to flourish in New York, growing stronger rather than breaking down in this age of mass communication and uni-fit lives, is two-fold. First, New York has a wonderfully heterogenous mix of people, people who love their cultures and work hard to preserve their heritage. That's fitting. New York, after all, is the funnel that filled this country's melting pot.

Second, the range of the land in New York — in distance and topography — is incredibly expansive. Consider: Manhattan is on a latitude with Eureka, California while Rouses Point, on the Canadian border, is as far north as Minneapolis and as far away from, say, Jamestown, as Chicago is from West Virginia. Or think about this: On a moonlight August night while two lovers stroll the beaches of South Hampton, a pair of hardy mountaineers may be bivouaced on the summit of an Adirondack peak in a foot or more of snow.

New York just exceeds the physical and metaphorical boundaries of a state. New York, simply put, is an empire unto its own.

All this makes a book about New York a challenging undertaking. How can one show the diversity of the state in a way that appeals to all

New Yorkers? What holds such a book together? Can there be some invisible, unifying thread that stitches the state's borders?

I think there is, and I think it exists here in the vision of a man. Clyde Smith, who is a good friend of long standing, has a unique eye. Clyde can look at the familiar and see the unusual. He can wait for that moment when the mundane becomes sublime. Without gimmicks, without cliches, without being avant garde or bizarre, Clyde can find stunning beauty where few would believe it might exist.

He does that here, page after page, and in so doing I think he pulls that unseen thread to unify the portrait of a very divergent state. At least he does for me. The cohesive element here is the view and the light with which this man records beauty in every inch of New York. In the big scene and the small. From the air and six inches off the ground. In winter and summer, spring and fall. On lakes and rivers, mountains, woods and city streets. Even the familiar radiates with a vitality we normally find only in the unknown. The pictures of places I know so well are as spectacular here as those of areas of New York I have never seen.

Not to say one man's eye can homogenize New York to some bland pap. No, but *this* man's eye can distill and clarify and illuminate the spectacles of the state so that without mawkish sentimentality, a man from Buffalo can appreciate and find pride in the rest of his state. . . . In the rest of his Empire.

Lionel Atwill

Orient village and cultivated fields, Orient Point.   Windmill, Gardiners Island.

Snow geese on Long Island.

Boating activity in Great South Bay near Robert Moses Causeway, Fire Island.

Overleaf: Montauk Point Light, tip of Long Island.

Sag Harbor, Long Island. Dunes at Eatons Neck, Long Island Sound. 17

Montauk harbor, Lake Montauk and entrance to Block Island Sound.

Dunes and erosion control fence, South Hampton.   *Overleaf:* Lower tip of Manhattan, Financial District, Battery Park and World Trade Center.

Financial District and East River from top of World Trade Center.   Empire State Building, George Washington Bridge looking uptown from World Trade Center.

Saint Patrick's Cathedral, 5th Avenue.

Christmas tree, Rockefeller Center.

Overleaf: Central Park, Plaza Hotel.

Harlem River and bridges looking down Manhattan.

Pan Am Building and Park Avenue.

Apartment houses along Sutton Place.

Girl walking her rabbit in Central Park.

Overleaf: South Street Seaport Museum and East River.

Christmas display, Rockefeller Center.

Park Avenue looking south toward Pan Am Building.

Overleaf: Midtown, United Nations Building and others. Hudson River in distance.

Fountain, Grand Army Plaza, Central Park South and 5th Avenue. Christmas display, Park Avenue near Chemical Bank and New York Trust Company.

Entrance to Brooklyn Bridge, Manhattan side of East River.

View of Financial District across East River from Brooklyn.

Overleaf: Bear Mountain Bridge and Hudson River.

West Point Military Academy and view up Hudson River.

Pass and review of the colors at West Point Military Academy.

Overleaf: Antique planes from Old Rhinebeck Aerodrome, Rhinebeck.

Castle Rock on the Hudson opposite West Point.

Shawangunk Mountains, Minnewaska State Park.

Fox Hunt, Millbrook.

Aerial view of Canada geese near Poughkeepsie.

Overleaf: Late light on rural Adirondack road.

Adirondack forest.

Great Northern Loon "walks on water," Upper St. Regis Lake.

Geese at Wadhams.

Gosling, Toulouse species.   *Overleaf:* Adirondack Peaks, Mt. Marcy the highest (left), Algonquin (right) and Great Range (foreground).

Whiteface Mountain, Lake Placid.

Whiteface Mountain Ski Area.

Changing colors on Lake Champlain.

Young hawk with breakfast.

Overleaf: The Great Range of the Adirondacks.

Split Rock Falls near Elizabethtown, Adirondacks.

St. Regis canoe region, Adirondacks.

Cascade Lakes near Lake Placid.　　　　Ice cutters on Cascade Lakes.　　　　*Overleaf:* Adirondack farm.

Vernon Pierce and Harold Sayre at auction in Whallonsburg.

Spring apple.

OK Slip Falls in the remote Upper Hudson River Gorge.

Heron lifts off lake at dawn. *Overleaf:* Dawn on Lake Champlain, Westport harbor marina.

Cliffs on Pokamoonshine Mountain, Adirondacks.   Henry Goff and son June Goff using old planer.   81

Wadhams, United Church of Christ.

Lake Champlain ferry crosses from Vermont to Essex.   *Overleaf:* Albany, Empire State Plaza with view toward State Capitol.

Fort Ticonderoga on Lake Champlain.

Village of Wells Bridge in Susquehanna River Valley.   Catskills.   *Overleaf:* Fogbound ocean-going ship on St. Lawrence Seaway.

Power lines and towers near Massena.   Russian freighter passes through Eisenhower lock at Massena.

Steuben Glass engraving, "Butterfly Girl" at Corning.

Finger Lakes Race Track.

Buck Dodge farm near Palmyra.

Overleaf: Village of Virgil near Cortland.

Taughannock Falls near Ithaca and Cayuga Lake.   Cazenovia.

Grape picker, Westfield, on Lake Erie.

East side of Keuka Lake near Penn Yan. Vineyards, orchids and corn.   *Overleaf:* Niagara Falls.

Niagara Falls. Ice formations along Niagara River above falls.

Dawn, Niagara Falls.

In flight over frozen Niagara Falls.

Overleaf: Niagara Falls.

Buffalo, on Lake Erie.

Old ship 'Canadian' raised from bottom of lake now on display in Buffalo.

Amish farm near Panama.

Amish farming.

Hurricane Mountain, Adirondacks.